W9-BFE-650

A SURVIVAL GUIDE FOR TODAY'S TEENS

IBSN: **978-1-4357-1747-3**

JERRY WEICHMAN, PH.D

TABLE OF CONTENTS

INTRODUCTION

Being a young adult can really suck.

I mean, think about it: No matter how good or bad things are, the bottom line is that you are old enough to do your own thing but you still have to listen to parents and teachers. You are not a kid anymore, but you are still not free to be the adult you know you can and will become. On top of that, there is so much juvenile, cliquey, dramatic crap going on in high school. People are trying to be "the man" or the "queen bee" and are putting up a front like they've got it all together and everything is O.K. People tease and gossip like crazy. The simple reality is that most people your age really don't know who they are, where they're going, or what they'll become. Most teens feel totally insecure and inadequate. In addition, they tend to dump on others in order to feel better. A lot of people judge books by their covers in high school. You are often not seen for who you really are or for who you will be. You are either in or you are out. And the "in" crowd seems to get smaller and more exclusive for the people that even care enough to want to be included in the first place. It sucks!

No matter how things are for you right now, I feel your pain, your struggle, your conflict, your anger. You may feel trapped or stuck right now. You may feel helpless, hopeless and that things are always going to be this way. I sure did.

As I sit here writing this, I am not that much older than you. I have just come from where you are going (college, graduate school, and the real world) and I can tell you that what's out there is awesome. Things will not always be this way and what you've got going on is more than likely the usual challenges of high school and being a teen. But guess what? It's temporary. You can and will be validated as the person you know you are by society and the people close to you in life. Once you make it through high school, I swear it really does get better!

This book is a description of some of my personal struggles as a teen and young adult, and the tools that I have used to become successful in many different aspects of my life. During college, I achieved academic awards for psychology, played Division I football, was president of my fraternity house, and received a doctorate by the age of 26. Oh, and by the way, I did all this while completely bombing my SATs and without a right foot!

I have compiled everything I have learned on **how to deal** with life – and deal with it successfully – in this book. You can pick and pull from it and add it to your life. You can learn **how to deal** with what's going on right now. You can learn how to elevate your mood and feel better regardless of what you are currently dealing with - even family and peer problems. Better yet, you can learn from (and laugh at) my mistakes and misfortunes. Being that I have just come from where you are going, much of what is described here will help you through high school, college, working in the real world or just with life in general.

Make no mistake, though. No one can apply these tools for you. This is your journey and you make the choices in your life. It is important for you to understand that you are the only driver of your car in life and no matter what I say, what your parents say, what your teachers or anybody else says, you are the one behind the wheel. Part of being an adult is grabbing onto your steering wheel, taking control of your car, and slamming the gas so that you haul butt! So sit back, grab on and let's roll...

Accepting Myself

I'm a licensed clinical psychologist specializing in young adults. I have a private practice in Newport Beach, California. I've worked with teens in substance abuse programs and I'm a motivational speaker at high schools and middle schools. But I wasn't always this secure and successful; things were tough for me growing up.

When my mom was pregnant with me, she developed some health issues and the doctor at the time told her she'd lose the baby if she didn't take the medicine he prescribed. What he failed to tell her was that it could cause birth deficiencies in babies. So to make being a kid even more difficult, when I was born, I had a right foot with no bones in it and a deformed, small left foot with only three toes. They had to amputate my right foot when I was an infant so that I could eventually be fitted with a prosthetic leg.

I felt like having a prosthetic leg was like a death sentence for me when I was young. Even as a kid, I saw how people picked on others for what was different or not right. I knew that I'd get teased if I didn't keep my disability on the down low.

So I wore pants. All. The. Time.

Even toward the end of school, when summer was coming and everybody was wearing their summer clothes in the 90-degree heat, there I was in pants. Kids would look at me and ask, "Dude, aren't you hot?" I'd say, "No," as I wiped beads of sweat from my forehead. Of course I was hot, but I was more concerned about keeping my secret and fitting in.

The one cool thing about my fake leg was that I could kick the heck out of any type of ball. Kicking with my prosthesis was like swinging a club. I could crush a ball. I was "the man" at elementary school kickball. The kids nicknamed me Bazooka because no matter how far the outfielders backed up, I could always kick the ball over their heads. I was a kickball god and it felt great because people gave me respect.

So it's the middle of third grade and as usual, I'm playing kickball. I come up to the plate with runners on base. The outfielders start dropping back, awaiting yet another booming kick from Bazooka. I see the ball rolling to me and I absolutely crush it. But then I felt something weird...something I'd never felt before. I look to the outfield, and the centerfielder is covering his head like a bowling ball was falling out of the sky. I looked up, saw the ball, and then I saw that there was something flying to the right of the ball. It took me a half of a second to figure out what the hell it was.

IT WAS MY FOOT, INSIDE MY SHOE, FLYING THROUGH THE AIR!

I looked down and sure enough, I was wearing my leg, but there was no foot or shoe attached to it. Let me help you understand what this was like: Can you imagine if one day in class, some guy you thought you knew stood up to ask the teacher a question and homeboy's arm drops off in front of everybody? You'd be freaking out right? The kids on the playground were FREAKING out, running for their lives, avoiding my foot like it was a puddle of puke and screaming, "Jerry's foot just came off! Jerry's foot just came off!"

It was mass mayhem. Two girls were in the corner, holding onto each other and crying. Teachers came out of their classrooms. The P.E. teacher came out, looked to his right and saw me sitting at home plate. He looked to his left and saw my foot in center field. You could see that he was trying to figure out how to get me to the nurse's office. So, he went into his shed, pulled out a dolly, which was basically a plank of wood with four wheels and a rope, rolled up to me and put me on top of it. Then, he rolled me out to center field to retrieve my foot. When we got there, he picked it up and placed it on top of my chest like it was my new baby that I had just delivered before wheeling me in front of EVERYBODY to the nurse's office. Now I know you've had some embarrassing school moments in your life, but story might win out (seriously, contact me if you have one that's worse).

Sure enough, the next day when I returned to school, the teasing started. People were calling me "peg leg," and all that stuff. But I started to figure out how to deal with it. I would just go with it and start to bag on my self. "Yup, I'm a peg leg pirate. Arrr matey."

When I was done, I would stick out my thumb like, "Yeah dude, you are cool, buddy. Right on." People, including the bullies, would just look at me in astonishment. See, people that tease are looking for someone who they can make feel bad so they can feel better. By reacting like they managed to get under your skin, you are helping them insult you. They don't get the same satisfaction with someone who plays it off or tries to ignore them.

HOW TO DEAL WITH A BULLY

When I talk about how emotions work later in the book, you'll see that the people who tease or bully – or for girls, gossip – are not big, intimidating, angry people. They're actually people who are quite hurt, feel small and don't know how to deal with the negativity in their lives. See them for who they really are! It's a lot easier to see someone who's trying to inflict pain on you as a victim that you pity, rather than an intimidating force. You have no idea what's going on in their life. They might come from an abusive family where they're teased or beaten by their parents or sibling. They may have been molested or someone close to them may have recently died. You just never know what is really going on with bullies, but know for sure that things aren't good for them.

Now just because they are hurting doesn't mean that you should just let it go. Try talking with them first. If that approach fails and the bullying continues, then you should tell an administrator (usually the assistant principal). I know that is seems you are telling on someone, right? I talk about trying to find a positive in every negative situation in a later chapter, but I can tell you this now: If there was a positive to the Columbine shootings, as well as all the other school shootings, it's that there is a no-bullying policy in schools across the nation. Administrators don't want bullying and teasing to get out of control and turn into something worse, so they put their foot down on it. If you and/or your parent were to talk to the administrators and let them know what's up, they will bring that person into the office to be punished. If that individual were to come back to you for retaliation then all you have to do is tell the same administrator again. You know the saying "the squeaky wheel gets the oil?" If that administrator found out that the same thing happened again, even greater action will be taken. I've seen kids expelled and arrested. A plus to this is that you don't have to drop to their level or get physical with them to get the situation resolved.

Everybody gets crap from other people in school. It's almost like a right of passage. No doubt, it sucks ... really sucks.

Once I moved into middle school (BTW, I did my internships at a middle and a high school, so I know kids are way harsher with each other in middle school than they are in high school), I was friends with this girl named Nadine.

Nadine was gorgeous. Red hair, light eyes, killer personality. A really cool, kicked back girl. Nadine was pretty much as good as it got at that age ... except she had a mole on her face. A lot of people have a moles or birthmarks on their face, but her mole was almost the size of a dime. One of the things that is so messed up with our society is that we're conditioned to pick out what's wrong, different or imperfect about others rather

than what is good or right. Being that everybody is different and that nobody is perfect, that is kind of messed up, right? I was in the same boat. I kept obsessing about her mole.

So I figured I'd roll up to Nadine and ask her about it one day at lunch. I walked up to her:

"Hey Jerry."

"Hey Nadine," I replied. "So what's up with that?"

"With what?" she replied.

"With that," I said (pointing at her face).

"With what?" she replied again.

All of the sudden I realized that she had absolutely no clue what I was talking about because she was comfortable with her face and everything that was on it. She was so chill with it that it made me O.K. with it and I didn't even feel the need to ask her about it anymore. Then I had one of those "light bulb" moments where I realized that I had made my leg situation worse for me and everybody around me by hiding it rather than just accepting myself.

Here's the deal: There are things that you might not like about yourself that you will never be able to change. This is what you are rolling into life with. The sooner you can find a way to be O.K. with EVERYTHING that you can't change about yourself, the easier life will be for you, the more confident you will become and the easier it will be for you to just hang out. I'm sure you know people at school who aren't the hottest or the tallest or the skinniest or the richest, but are still really popular with others and seem quietly confident. These are the people who have usually accepted themselves and aren't too concerned about what others say or whether people judge them.

This type of confidence is attractive to everyone in life. Accept yourself now. Embrace both your positive and negative attributes because they are YOU. Life will be much easier.

Next up was high school. Now, there are good things about high school but for the purposes of learning **how to deal** I want to focus on what isn't good about it. If you are having a good time in high school, that's sweet! If you are not, believe me when I say that you are in the majority. One thing I have realized that after working with teens for so many years, is that there are a ton of people at school in the same boat as you. The thing is that nobody really talks about it. Everybody tries to put up a front like everything is fine and they've got it all together.

As I talked about earlier, I hated how a ton of people try to be "the man" or the "queen bee." People tease or gossip like crazy. It's like a one-person operator game. You know that game when you were a kid where you stand in a circle and one person starts with a statement and it is passed around by everyone and completely changed by the end? This is how bad gossip in high school is, except with gossip, everyone changes the content!
Nobody really knows who they are, where they're going, or what they'll become. Because of this most

teens feel totally insecure and inadequate and usually dump on others to feel better. Many people sell out to run with the popular crowd. You know who I'm talking about. They change their looks, sacrifice grades and do drugs just to fit in. They lose their focus on life and themselves in the process. A lot of people judge books by their covers. You are rarely seen for who you really are or who you have the potential to become. It feels like you are either in or you are out. And the "in" crowd seems to get smaller and more exclusive for the people that even care enough to want "in" in the first place.

When I was dealing with this myself, part of me felt helpless and hopeless. It felt as if life was always going to be like that for me. But I was so wrong. This is one message I want to drive home to you. Life is better outside of high school. More mature and better friendships, people who really see you, freedom. It is worth the time and the sacrifice. And in case no one has told you, everybody has to pay their dues in life.

One way you can look at high school and living at home is like it's a sacrifice you have to make in order to get ahead and move on. It's important that you accept that today is your temporary reality and try to make the most of it. Your whole life will not be this way. A few years after graduation, you won't know or talk to 99% of these people anyway. If you are looking for a way out or just want help doing better in school, read the next chapter.

School, School, School

Studying, Grades & College

Like I said before, I received academic honors for my psychology studies in college, I was president of a fraternity house, and I played Division I football, but prior to all of that I absolutely bombed my SATs! My score was HORRIBLE. Regardless, I got past my setbacks to achieve my goals. How I did all this is detailed in this book. And it is really easy. If I can accomplish all this with what I had going wrong for me at that point then there is no way you can't do the same.

I hope you want to go to college. You deserve the experience. First of all, you are finally free. Imagine doing whatever, wherever, whenever, with whomever. People are more mature and there is less of the people "not seeing you for who you are" dynamic. You meet a lot of people who are into the same things you are. Whatever your interests, college offers plenty of opportunities to learn about them. Not to mention, outside of class your new friends are road-tripping and the parties can be fun, too. College is the only time in life that all you have to do is study first and then you can go have fun. Nobody is telling you what to do or how to do it. Life is good. Most people say that this one of the best times in one's life. Why do you think movies like "Animal House" and "Old School" are so popular? Besides being funny, people love to revisit those carefree times.

Everybody is in a similar situation at college. They don't know many people and are happy to be on their own and it becomes really easy to socialize and meet people. It becomes even easier if you join a club, play a sport, join a fraternity or sorority or just get involved.

I not only made it on a Division I college football team but I made the traveling team, too (I was #2 out of 6 guys with the starter being an All-American.) It was an accomplishment for me. We traveled to so many noteworthy schools. Nebraska, Arizona,

Oregon, Louisiana. Different colors, different stadiums, different weather, different fans and students. I remember running onto the field at Nebraska with 90,000 screaming fans so loud, I couldn't get the noise out of my helmet and thinking that this experience was what I had always dreamed about as a kid. Here I was, living one of my dreams.

I also joined a fraternity. I never ever pegged myself as a fraternity guy. My roommate convinced me to go through rush. Rush is a period of time when all the fraternities or sororities open their doors to you, take you through, explain their traditions, meet the members, go on fun outings. I was scared of pledging and all the things we hear about it. I remember a bro putting his arm around me during rush and pointing to his significantly overweight brother in the house and telling me, "If this guy can make it through pledging, anyone can." So I went through the process. And I was really glad I did. I learned a lot about myself and made a lot of lifelong friends in the process.

To make a long story short, I ended up becoming so much closer to fifty guys who had my back and I got to learn a lot about myself by being so close with them. We traveled and I got to know their families and see where many of them grew up. I became president and learned a lot about dealing with the college administration. I could write a book just about my college experience so I'll cut this short. Basically, whatever your interests may be, what I want you to know is that college is a great time to get involved, learn about life and discover what you're all about.

.

You don't have to know what you want to be in life to go to college. You don't usually even have to declare a major until your sophomore year. You know how in high school you either get to pick ceramics or photography? In college, you get to pick from tons of classes that all count towards graduation. I took intro to biology, psychology and sociology just to get a flavor of what was my style.

And get this: You don't even have to have money to go to college. You can take out grants or student loans. Did you know that there are programs where the government pays for all four years of your college without asking for any money during that time and then, when you graduate and start making $40,000-$60,000 a year with a college degree, you pay them back as little as $50-$100 a month?

What you do need – simply because it makes getting into college a lot easier – is to do well in school now. Grades don't have to be perfect – just good. Consider it the price of admission for college.

You don't have to change up much in your life to do well in school. You can still be the same person and do well in school at the same time. You just have to study. Studying isn't really that hard. If you have decent time-management and organizational skills, then it becomes pretty easy.

O.K., let's be honest: Homework sucks, right? I absolutely hated almost every single second of it. I mean, there are so many other things that are more enjoyable than doing homework when you get out of school. Watching T.V., IMing friends, posting stuff on MySpace or Facebook , talking on the phone, playing video or computer games, surfing the Internet, kicking back with friends, going surfing, skating and shopping are all definitely more enjoyable than doing homework.

Here's the deal though: When I was your age, I was not enjoying living at home, let alone having to spend most of my waking hours amongst the people I was going to high school with. I realized that I wanted to get the hell out after graduation so I would not be living at home any longer than I needed to be and so I could go start a life for myself.

I realized that what you do in high school with your grades today will affect your shot at college which later affects your job and in turn your job affects your money and we all know that your money affects a lot of the comforts of life. So essentially, because of that, what you are doing right now is directly affecting your future life as a 20-, 30-, or even 60-year-old. Imagine that right now your future self is looking down the line at you. Are you saying, "Sweet, we're hooked up!"? Or is it more like, "Um, are you kidding me?"

What you have to see is that what you do in the next one to six years (depending on what grade you are currently in) directly affects the next seventy years of your life. Pretty crazy, huh? Now some of you might come from a family that is loaded and you might be thinking, "No big deal, I'll just mooch off of Mom and Dad, live at home and not do too much."

The problem with that is that YOU have a specific purpose on this planet and a special gift to give to the world. If you don't go out and figure out who you really are, what your gift and purpose is on this planet, then you'll feel lost throughout your life. Life speaks to you if you pay attention and when you are not where you are supposed to be in your life, you feel it. It feels like things are off. You feel it in your stomach, heart and mind. People who are lost in life often get easily irritated and sometimes angry. This is because life speaks to each of us. When you find your path and who you are, it feels really good because you feel comfortable and confident in yourself, in life, and in the direction you are going.

Here is the bottom line: Ask yourself, "Do I want to live at home with your parents the rest of your life while everybody else is leaving for college and going to have a killer time?"

If you answer is "NO!" then you have to talk the talk and walk the walk now. Your grades are your only guaranteed way to become successful. Yes, it is possible to become successful without a college degree, but the odds are stacked against you from the beginning. Pulling grades is like insurance. No matter what you want to become (athlete, actor, etc.) if you go to college and get a degree, you will always have a decent job that pays well to fall back on if your career of choice falls apart.

In addition to this, your grades are like your credit score when you are a young adult. In life, if you have a good credit score, you can have anything you want (like cars and houses) and people are dying to sell them to you at great rates. Your grades are like this right now for you. If you have good grades, you can approach your parents with so much more leverage and often times, get what you want. Raise your credit score.

So, as you think about studying, let me ask you a question: If you are running a race and the race coordinator gives you the choice of running the steep hill section or the flat section first, which one would you choose? Most people would pick the steep first. When asked why they say, "Because my legs are the freshest so I'd tackle the hill then coast the rest of the race."

Homework is not much different. We all know it sucks but it has to get done. Because you've been in school all day (whether you've been paying attention or not), your brain has been chewing on information for hours on end. The freshest you will be in order to tackle that "hill" is right when you get home from school, whether you get home at 3 p.m. or 7 p.m. after a practice or work. To make your life the easiest for yourself, your homework should always be done first, then use what you enjoy (T.V., videogames, IMing) as your reward for completion of your work. One of the biggest problems that I see is that teens come home from school and go right to doing what they enjoy the most. After you get a taste of the good stuff who in their right mind would want to go back to something less enjoyable? No one would. In fact, you are actually putting a bad taste in your brain's mouth.

Imagine that you are sitting at the dinner table eating broccoli, steak, and a big piece of chocolate cake. You are not allowed to leave until it is all finished. If you participate in enjoyable activities before doing homework, it would be like having half of the chocolate cake first, then going and eating broccoli and steak. It doesn't sound good right? That's because it's not in the right progressive order to taste good. You need to have that similar progressive order with your responsibilities so that things in your life "taste right."

Some of you might be able to sit down and do your homework but then get distracted. You are sitting there and all of a sudden this voice creeps up in your head: "Hey, you've had a hard day. Why don't you just take a break? Just 15 or 20 minutes. You've already done a few assignments, the others can wait. Just jump on the computer, call a friend, or watch some T.V."

You start to think to yourself, "Yeah, I have had a hard day. Yeah, I do deserve a break." Then what happens? You take the break and that 15-20 minutes becomes an hour or two and then you realize that, "Oh no! It's late and I'm nowhere near done with my work." Then you either stress out and stay up late to get it done or you show up to school empty handed. Promising to wake up early the next morning and get it done rarely works.

I had a professor in grad school say that delayed instant gratification is one of the truest tests of an adult. It means that you can delay doing what you want so that you can take care of your responsibilities and then utilize what you wanted to do as your reward. Kids do what they want to do. Adults do what they need to do, and then do what they want as their reward.

Right now, you might be in between a kid and an adult and the two might equally exist in you. You've got to tell yourself the "why" behind everything. If you haven't figured this one out yet, let me help you. When you are on top of your school work, you feel better about yourself, you are more optimistic about your future, you usually get your parents off your back and you typically get more rewards out of life. These are the "whys" that you need to tell the lazy side of yourself that wants you to take a break.

See, everybody has a lazy side and that's O.K. You just have to talk to that voice or thought inside of you when it creeps up. When you are done with your adult responsibilities, that kid is going to be able to do whatever he or she wants. Work first, and then utilize what you like to do as the reward.

The bigger problem here is that if you are being distracted by cell phones, video games and computers right now, you are going to have huge problems later on in life. In college and in the real world you are going to have friends knocking on your door and even more distracting and enjoyable activities. You absolutely have to work first and then play. This is exactly how I was able to be successful in high school, college and even now. In college, I would go to the library after my classes were done and sit there – whether it was one hour or five hours – until my work was done and I was ready for the next class. My reward was doing what I wanted with the time I had left. Right now, I love working with young adults, but I'd rather be surfing, snowboarding, mountain biking, hiking with the dog or spending time with my wife. I take care of my responsibilities (for me it is work, for you it's probably chores and homework) and then I reward myself later by going surfing or snowboarding. It's really that simple.

Here are some easy study techniques for you to help you get schoolwork done well with less time:

WRITE IT DOWN

You typically have a 10- to 30-page chapter to read every night with a test at the end of the week or two. There is a lot of information in there that you know and information that you don't know. As you read the first chapter, get out a lined piece of paper and write down everything that you don't know. This helps you remember it better because it takes it from the book to your eyes, into your brain, out through your hand and onto your paper. When you are done doing that, label it and file it away. The next night, do it again and then paper clip the two chapters together. When it comes time to study for the test, you have "trimmed the fat" in that you have everything that you need to study and don't have to over-stuff your brain with information that you already know. On top of that, it is in your own handwriting, which means that your brain receives the information better.

REMEMBER WHEN YOU ARE FRESHEST

Start with your hardest or least enjoyable subject first and work towards the easiest or most enjoyable one. If you do it the other way around, it is an uphill battle. If you were on a bike, blades or skateboard, you'd rather start at the top (the hardest) and ride your way downhill rather than up it.

LIMIT DISTRACTIONS

It has been proven that the less distracted you are, the better you can concentrate. When you can concentrate, you increase your effectiveness and ability to focus. In turn, you will be more successful. Don't take phone calls, texts or IMs until your assignments are done. It will make you work harder to get things done if you discipline yourself.

TAKE SMALL STEPS

Many teens focus on all the stuff they have to do or get done and stress themselves out to the point that they can't even begin to study or don't know where to begin. This happens in life when there is a lot on your plate and it will happen many more times throughout life. Think about eating a steak. Have you ever sat down and tried to cram an entire steak down your throat? Of course not. You cut it into bite-size pieces and eat it one piece at a time until it's done. It is the same with your work. Rank what is the most important or what needs the most immediate attention and cut that piece off and just focus on that one piece. Don't allow yourself to look at or think about all the other stuff or the rest of the steak. Focus on chewing and swallowing that one piece first. Then, cut another piece and focus on that one.

STAY ORGANIZED WITH YOUR STUFF, ASSIGNMENTS AND YOUR TIME

There is so much going on in your busy life. I was always stressed out when I tried to keep everything I wanted or needed to get done in my head. I was stressed because I didn't want to forget anything and with so much going on, something was always left out. Then I was even more stressed. I began using an organizer and it made all the difference for me. I started with an old school organizer book and eventually upgraded to a PDA. I would take all of my daily homework assignments and put them down. I'd also take any due dates of future tests, quizzes or reports, practices, appointments, friend's birthdays, parties or kickbacks and put them down, as well.

All of a sudden, I had everything that I was stressing about organized and out of my head. I could stress when I wanted to by picking my calendar up, but could also put it down and not worry. I'd check it before I left school to make sure I had all the books I needed for the day and head home. When I got home, I took my calendar out, organized my assignments from hardest (or least enjoyable) to easiest (and most enjoyable). Every time I completed an assignment, I would cross it off my calendar. Crossing things off feels good. It also makes you feel good to take care of your business and see what you've accomplished when you are done.

ENCOURAGE YOURSELF

You are going to need to develop a voice inside of you that is supportive and encouraging. Not just to get you through homework assignments, but for everything that you do in life. There are a lot of different personalities inside of you and everyone else. We're not schizophrenic. There is the son/daughter you, the sibling you, the boyfriend/girlfriend you, the student you, the athlete you, the musician you. The voice inside of you that has been encouraging, strong and resilient throughout your life is the voice that you need to call upon to help you get through tasks.

Encourage yourself the same way you would root for your own child at a soccer game, "Come on! You can do it! That's it, you are almost there! Keep it up!" If you can talk to yourself like this, you are going to notice that you get a lift it and you actually accomplish things much better. You are going to need to do this throughout your whole life.

When you accomplish each task, pat yourself on the back. Seriously. Be the encouraging and supportive person that you wished you had as a kid. The more you can encourage and reward yourself, the more successful you will be.

ATTEND CLASS AND PAY ATTENTION

So many young adults ditch class, or when in class, they screw around with friends or their cell phones. I understand. It can be SO boring. But your teacher doesn't get paid much and is only there because they care about giving you an education. If you are not there mentally, you don't know what is going on and you fall behind. If you screw around, it is going to upset your teacher and it will lower your grade regardless of if you are doing well. Have you ever given a presentation where people don't pay attention? This is what your teachers go through every period of every single day.

If you pay attention, attend class, and show that you are trying, most teachers will notice and give you the benefit of the doubt when it is time to fill out report cards. Plus if you are not in class, you may not understand the information as well, which will affect your homework and test-taking skills and will ultimately affect your grade. Paying attention helps the time pass rather than looking at the clock every two minutes.

There are so many "I can't believe that I'm doing this right now" experiences in college. I hope that you do not miss out on the opportunity. Remember, you neither have to know what you want to do nor have money. You just have to not want to live at home with mom and dad when you graduate high school, you have to want a good life, and you have to want it all bad enough to work for it right now, pull grades and go start YOUR life.

WHAT HAPPENED TO THE PARTY?

By the end of college, I had my fraternity brothers, the guys on the football team, people I met around school, professors who have invited me to their house, administrators I developed a close bond with and, most importantly, my girlfriend (who eventually became my wife) who was a year behind me in school.

I left them all behind to move to Orange County, California, where I really didn't know anybody. I moved into a second floor apartment and all of a sudden, I started having pain at the bottom of my amputated leg. I saw a doctor who told me that because I never had support on the bottom of my leg inside of my prosthesis and because of playing football, the skin had began to stretch around the end of the bone and was going to tear if I didn't get corrective surgery.

So I got the surgery. They sawed off the tip of my bone so that they could move more supportive skin underneath. Talk about nerve pain. It was the first time in my life that I wasn't wearing my prosthesis and I felt naked. I remember the first time I ran errands with my crutches and no foot. I walked into the bank with my pant leg folded and pinned up on my pants so it wouldn't drag on the ground. The bank was packed and from across the room a little kid pointed at me and yelled, "Look Mommy, that man has no leg!"

Have you ever seen those scenes in movies when everybody in the place stops what they are doing and stares at one guy? That's what happened. I remember thinking to myself, "Well, this is what I'm rolling with so I'll just make the best of it." So I tried to do just that. I had to figure out how to do laundry, which was on the first floor, and go grocery shopping literally with no leg to stand on. It was tough.

I was supposed to take one month to recover. A few weeks later, I got the stitches out and knew something was wrong when the doctor said, "Uh oh," as he was removing my stitches. The skin was stretched so tight that when he removed the stitches, the whole incision popped wide open. I wasn't bleeding, which would have been a good thing, so he wasn't sure if the skin was good or alive. He told me to wait a few more weeks to see if it was going to close up. I was dying not because of pain but because I wanted to get my leg back so that I could return to my life. So much of my life had been halted or impeded. I was starting to get run down.

A few weeks later the doctor looked at it again and told me that I had to go back into surgery in a few weeks to fix what had happened. So I got the surgery...again. They had to cut the skin further down until it bled, which meant it was alive and it was going to heal. It hurt so bad. My leg was wrapped in a cast and I was still struggling to go to grad school, deal with the stares and trying to get my life back.

A month or so later, it was time to get my cast off. The doctor cut the cast off, took one look, and gave me what was now his standard statement, "Uh oh." He proceeded to tell me that my leg had become severely infected. If the infection had reached the bone, more of my leg was going to have to be removed. I couldn't believe it. After cleaning what he could, he told me that although the infection was severe, it hadn't reached the bone. I was going to have to just let it heal itself and it was going to take many more months.

The doctor left the room for a second to get something to help clean my leg. I looked down at my leg to survey my situation. Not only was the open incision still there, but the infection had eaten up the flesh inside and I could pretty much see the bone. I completely lost it. I had already fought this thing for more than eight months and there I was even further behind where I had started. I cried while lying on the table and looked up at the ceiling and yelled, "Why?!? Why is this happening to me?" "What did I do?" I was talking directly to my maker and had absolutely no idea why something like this was happening to a guy like me who was a decent person and just wanted to go out and help people in life. Nothing made sense. Life seemed dark and bleak.

After fighting my situation and the pending depression for eight months, I gave in and temporarily, I gave up. In my practice, I have worked before with really depressed teens who describe seeing everything in life in black and white rather than in color. At that moment, I totally understood what they had meant. I started to get really depressed. If you haven't been depressed before, here is what to look for in your life or in the friends and family that surround you:

- Changes in your sleep patterns. You start to sleep too much or too little. I started to sleep less. I had so much trouble falling asleep. At 1:00, 2:00, 4:00 in the morning, I was still awake. This threw my sleeping pattern off and started waking up at noon feeling really unrested.

- Your appetite changes. You start to eat too much or too little. Personally, I lost my appetite. Before the surgery, I was 185 pounds. At my lowest point in my depression, I weighed 155. I couldn't believe that I was in the 150s but I just couldn't eat. I had absolutely no appetite. Small meals made me full and I had to force myself to eat because, though I was depressed, I still wanted to stay alive. My eyes were sunken in my face and there were large black circles underneath them.

- You don't have a lot of energy and you feel kind of bored a lot of the time.

- You become socially isolated. You don't go outside much for anything. I didn't have much energy and I didn't really want to leave my apartment. I just wanted to stay inside and do nothing. I had the "screw-its."

- You get body aches. Depressed people often have headaches, stomach aches, backaches, neck pain and shoulder pain with no medical explanation for them.

- You don't find pleasure in normally enjoyable activities. Seeing people I cared about or doing activities I enjoyed just didn't have the same affect on me. Though I felt better doing them, it was definitely not the same level of enjoyment.

- You get sensitive to rejection and failure and you also feel helpless now and hopeless about the future. I saw no end in sight and no light at the end of the tunnel.

If you or the people around you are exhibiting the symptoms above, say something. Get whoever it is help. Depressed people do not usually have the energy to take the initiative to get the help they need. Suicidal people typically hint about killing themselves a time or two before attempting it.

I was obviously really depressed. I had no food in my apartment because I couldn't go grocery shopping and I was sick of drive-through meals. The only positive thing during that period was when an old fraternity brother drove an hour to my apartment and took me grocery shopping. This guy helped pick stuff out for me that I wanted and needed, loaded it up in the car, went to my apartment and carried $350 worth of groceries up to the second floor in one trip! When people are there for you in your time of need, they appear more like angels sent from heaven than people. Doing small things for people in life goes a long way.

As I said before, you are the driver of your car in life. In order to change anything in your life, you either have to be sick enough of your situation to do something about it or you have to be at rock-bottom so that there is nowhere for you to go but up. I think that my situation was a combination of the two. I sat there going, "Come on Jerry. You are so over this. You know a lot about life and psychology. What are some things that you could do to make yourself feel better REGARDLESS of whether this situation changes or not?" These tools are what are outlined in the next couple of chapters.

Before you read the next chapter, I want to address something important. I was sitting there depressed, and had no idea why that was happening to me. My answer was soon to follow. When I felt better, I had a new outlook on life. I knew what it was like to be depressed and could relate when I had a depressed client. From those experiences, I created a presentation about the tools that I developed to pull me out of depression. This enabled me to become a motivational speaker to young adults. It really put me on my path in life. I want to propose to you that things in life happen for a reason. There are no accidents. The challenges that are placed in front of us are meant for us to learn from and overcome. They help guide us to who we are supposed to be or what we are supposed to do in life. The saying that what doesn't kill you makes you stronger is so true.

You've already been through some difficult times in life and you are stronger as a result of going through them. Life speaks to you if you pay attention. Listen to your intuition, your gut. That subtle thought or feeling in your stomach will always lead you in the right direction and away from trouble. Look for the meanings or lessons in things. If you don't learn from your experiences, you are bound to make the same mistakes. Once you figure it out and change accordingly, life will change with you and you will be in a better place. Look for the meanings. Look for the lessons. Listen to what life is trying to say to you.

Like I said, the tools that helped me figure out how to deal can help you too. If you use them in combination, you will feel at least a little better even if your situation stays the same or even if gets worse. After using these tools, my depression began to lift. I could almost feel the 100-pound plate on my shoulders lift up and off. I began to see life in color again. It is amazing how much you appreciate the simple things in life, like walking or feeling good, when they have been ripped away from you and you are lucky enough to get them back. I have a new-found appreciation for so many simple things in life. I'm now grateful that I went through all that.

FEELING BETTER: PHYSIOLOGICAL TOOLS

MOVE YOUR BODY

The first thing I did to pull myself out of my depression was to start getting daily exercise. If you go to a psychologist, psychiatrist or family physician, one of the first things they will recommend is to get on a workout program. Endorphins are released as your body responds to the physical stress of workouts and they serve to elevate your mood. When I was finally sick of being depressed, I started to take back control of my life. I started working out. I was doing cardio and weights at least four days a week. Go figure, I started feeling better almost immediately.

Get cleared by your doctor to workout and go hit it. On top of the endorphins, you can utilize all your anger or frustration and take it out on the weights or as you do cardio. As you workout, think about what is bothering you. The angrier you get, the harder you should push it. Get that feeling off of you.

There is also the psychological kick-back of taking care of yourself when you really need it. I would think to myself, "Here you go. You really need this and I'm hooking you up." On top of that, your body is mature enough, so that around six weeks into your workout program, you will get out bed one morning and see yourself in the mirror with some serious results. You will feel proud of your accomplishments and like you have that much more control over yourself and your life. You don't just have to workout in a gym to get the benefits I'm talking about. You can skate, go shopping with friends, walk the dog, surf, mountain bike -- anything that gets you moving. Plus as an added bonus, working out will usually help you sleep better too.

BON APPETIT!

I hated eating in the morning before school, but food is fuel for your car in life. Everybody gets low blood sugar, which lowers your mood. For some, it is two hours without food while for others it's six, but it happens to everyone. I wouldn't know why, but around lunch time, I would get agitated. Whenever I would eat, I would get this "AHH" feeling, almost like a warm wave coming over me. If the same thing happens to you, take note. That's your blood sugar elevating again. The minute you walk out the door without eating, your blood sugar begins to drop. Trying to make it through the day like that is like trying to drive 300 miles on a quarter tank of gas. It is just not happening.

During my depression, I didn't want to eat as much as I normally did and I felt more like crap as a result. So, because I was the one behind the wheel, I started to take control back of my life and eat something in the morning. I really couldn't eat so I would grab a protein shake or breakfast bar and charge it on the way to work. It gave me a foundation for the day and gave me the energy I needed to get through.

With regard to eating disorders (anorexia and bulimia), what is important to understand is that they are usually issues of control. Your life feels totally out of control so you try to control your body.

Here's the important thing that many teens don't know: There is a reason why there is no magic diet. Your brain always calculates a way around what you are trying to do.

If you restrict food for many hours or for a few days, your brain will yell down to your stomach, "Switch to survival mode!" In "survival mode" your metabolism slows down and the next time you eat again, whether it's a few hours or a few days, your body takes everything that comes down into your stomach and packs it away into fat storage because it never knows when food is going to come again. So you actually gain fat from restricting food. How can you feel better and lose fat at the same time? Start eating smaller meals (high in protein, if possible) five times a day. Something in the morning, something at lunch, a snack in the afternoon and dinner. When food comes regularly, your brain yells down to your stomach and tells it to speed your metabolism, everything goes right through you, you lose fat and you keep your blood sugar elevated as well.

PARTYING WILL CATCH UP TO YOU

Look, you've all heard the "just say no" stuff. I'm not here to tell you to do drugs and I'm not here to tell you not to use them. The bottom line is that if you haven't come in contact with drugs yet, you will eventually. Substance abuse is a prevalent element in today's society and it is one that's pretty serious. I'm not just talking about boozing (alcohol), blazing bowls (pot), doing lines (coke), rolling (ecstasy) or tweaking (meth); I'm talking about cigarettes and caffeine, too. Part of being a man or woman in the world is taking responsibility for yourself and understanding how things like drugs really affect you.

You have substances in your body called neurotransmitters (dopamine and serotonin) that make you feel happy and "high" through out the day. In a similar way to how your heart beats, your neurotransmitters are spit out into your blood stream and then some of it is sucked back up. Your body just keeps recharging and spitting out these neurotransmitters. When ever you feel high from smoking a bowl, doing a line, drinking or even smoking cigarettes or ingesting caffeine, it is because your body takes the neurotransmitters it has built up and dumps a ton of them into your blood stream all at one time. That is why you feel a high.

But what do you think happens a few hours or a day later? Your body now has a smaller amount of neurotransmitters to release into your blood stream. After the high, you get a low. You are left feeling worse than before. Thinking that you felt great a few hours ago, you decide maybe you'll do it again. What do you think happens? Less of a high, but more of a low afterwards. If you are doing this to avoid dealing with the hurt, pain and anger in your life, you should realize that you are making yourself more depressed. That would be like holding onto 25-pound weights while trying to swim. The more weight you add, the more you sink.

People who consistently abuse drugs like ecstasy are often permanently suppressing the receptor cites for neurotransmitters, and in effect, are making themselves more depressed throughout their entire life. I see this commonly in my practice. You have to go on anti-depressants for the rest of your life if you do major damage, and even then they don't always compensate for what you have lost.

The latest brain studies are also very telling. Research shows that the human brain continues to develop until around 25 years old. When drugs or alcohol are introduced to a developing brain, the brain will accommodate itself seek out those pleasures (because they release more dopamine) rather than conventional pleasures, such as happiness or success. Studies have shown that someone who starts drinking at 14 years or younger has around a 46% of developing an addiction in their lifetime. Someone who is 17 years has approximately a 24% chance while someone who is 21 years has only around a 9% chance of developing an addiction to alcohol in their lifetime. [1]

Many young adults that abuse substances have come into my office reporting that they feel like a piece of them is missing. I call this "the void." This often comes from unresolved difficult experiences in

---

[1] I know, I know...I hate these little footnotes, too. But this is the only one.

Source: Dr. Jeff Wilkins, Vice Chair of the Department of Psychiatry and Behavioral Neurosciences and Medical Director of Addiction Medicine, Cedars-Sinai Medical Center (Los Angeles, CA)

life. Using substances to fill this void is a mirage and will do nothing for you but to pull you down further. It is like a filling a hole in a tree trunk with a piece of Styrofoam. It provides no stability. One way to really fill "the void" is to deal with and express your feelings from experiences that have scarred you while learning to emotionally nurture yourself, which is described in the cognitive tools chapter under "parent yourself."

I also think that partying regularly is selfish. "I feel like this and I want to feel like this more." Life is about helping other people and giving. It's not all about you! What you give out, you get back. When you are wasted, you are into yourself and can't talk to people the way you normally do (which, by the way, kills your "game"). What's more, you'll find that you make the majority of the mistakes you make, such as saying or doing stupid things, occur in this state. If you can stop the substance abuse, it will make you feel more in control, better about yourself and less depressed and anxious.

The majority of sexual abuse and rapes that I hear about in my practice have happened to people who attended parties when one or both people were wasted. It is more common than you can even imagine.

SMILE

Seriously, I'm not kidding. When I was depressed, I felt better by forcing a smile even though I felt bad. It is kind of like the old saying, "Fake-it-'til-you-make-it."

Check this out, you've been smiling your whole life because of something funny or pleasurable that has happened. So now, after all these years of smiling, a conditioned response exists between the muscles in your face and the pleasure centers in your brain. Think to yourself, "I feel like crap." Feel the drop in your chest and stomach? Now smile (I'm serious), and think to yourself "I feel like crap." You don't feel the drop right? I force a smile when ever I'm not feeling quite like myself, or if I am in a bad mood or getting angry or sad and it often brings me back. Everybody can feel themselves getting more and more angry or sad. After a certain point if nothing is done about it, you can't pull yourself back out and you are stuck there for a while. Smiling definitely helps keep you from "falling off."

Soak Up the Sun

We're just like plants and we need sunlight to survive. We need a moderate amount of sunlight to feel good. Why? First, you get ultra-violet rays from the sun, which help lift your mood. Second, it is a great source of Vitamin D. Now, I'm not saying that you should go bake yourself. In fact, check with a doctor to make sure your skin is O.K.

The bottom line is that sitting inside and rotting when you are not happy is the worst thing to do. When I started getting out and getting sun, I immediately felt a little better. On top of that, I noticed that my skin cleared up when I was getting sun a few days a week. Anything that combines fun, sun and exercise will help hook you up in more ways than one.

Stand Up

Have you ever seen those people in life or at school who are walking while sulking, with their head down, dragging their feet? You can tell from across the room, street or yard that the person is having a horrible day, right? When I was feeling down, I would make a bigger effort to carry myself with pride. What I mean by that is that I would force myself to stand up straight, with my head up, chest out and shoulders back. No kidding, I started feeling better. This is another fake-it-'till-you-make-it tool.

As human beings, we are really into body language. We try to read everybody that we encounter in life. It is a survival mechanism. Is that person safe or dangerous? Happy or sad? Strong or weak? Could you imagine what our military would look like to other countries if we stood in line slouching with our shoulders forward and looking at the ground? Weak, unsure and unstable. That is how you come off to others when you do that.

ZZZZZZ's

Many young adults have trouble getting enough sleep. Most studies say that you should typically be getting about eight hours of sleep a night. Too much, you will be lethargic and lazy. Too little, you will feel run down, plus you will have a lowered immune system and can become sick and depressed. Your body is just like your cell phone or iPod. If you don't charge it up, it gives out on you.

If you are having trouble sleeping at night, it could be for a lot of reasons. Sometimes, it is your thoughts keeping you up at night. A lot of teenagers that I see in my practice talk about how they just keep "thinking about thinking" and very seldom reach any conclusions. Thoughts just keep spinning around and around their head. You need to give it an outlet or a place to go. What helped me was getting out a pad of paper and writing about everything that I was thinking and feeling. Write until you have nothing else to write about. It may be one piece or 20 pieces of paper. When you are done, shred it and throw it away. You don't need to see it nor does anyone else.

Some other helpful ideas:

- Take a hot shower or bath before bed. It relaxes your body. People say that it simulates the same warm environment as when you were in the womb. I don't know about that but regardless, it totally helps me out.

- Don't drink too much caffeine. You should have only 1-2 sodas a day or 1 cup of coffee. Be careful with energy drinks like Monster or Redbull. They have more caffeine than coffee or soda. It is like driving your car all over town in first gear. You'll burn it out eventually. If you get too wired, it's tough to come down for sleep.

- Keep your room cool. If feels naturally good for us to have it cold outside and warm under the sheets. If your room is too warm, it makes your core temperature rise and it is more difficult to sleep. Keep a wet washcloth next to the bed and wipe yourself down to cool off while trying to sleep.

- Get daily exercise. Like we discussed earlier, your body charges up as you sleep. If you don't drain your battery by getting exercise during the day and charge it back up with sleep at night, there is not going to be anymore charging to be done with sleep at night and your excess energy will keep you up and running.

- Limit the amount of stimulation before or during sleep. T.V., computer, video games, music, even the amount of light all play a part in keeping you up before bed. Limit them all, especially right before you crash.

- To help you fall asleep, think of your "soul food." What I mean by that is whatever the one place that you'd like to be or the one thing that you'd love to do for the rest of your life if you could. For me, it's definitely snowboarding. I love to strap on my snowboard and ride around God's backyard. If I could, I would love to do it every day for the rest of my life. What situation is like that for you? Focus only on using all of your senses of what it would be like to be there. What does it look like? What does it smell like? What does it sound like? What does it feel like? What does it taste like? Ask yourself this five times. The next thing you know, you'll be there and you can do what ever you want. The more you think of this (and only this), the farther away you will drift and the closer to sleep you will be.

If you have trouble sleeping and you are still up at like 3:00 or 4:00 in the morning, I recommend that you just stay up. I'm not kidding. Turn on the lights and start doing something entertaining. You will be tired in the early morning but will get a surge of energy later in the day and you will be more tired for bed that evening. Don't worry about catching up on sleep. Your body has the amazing ability to put you into a deeper sleep, even with less hours of it, to get you recharged for the next day.

If your problem is waking up in the morning, set your alarm clock on the opposite side of your room and crank it up. The minute your feet hit the floor to walk to the clock, it is stimulating for your body and will help you wake up enough so that you can keep yourself up. Just don't be weak and dive back into bed!

DEALING WITH STRESS

A majority of the teens I see in my practice today are too worked up and seriously stressed out. There are so many different stressors: parents, friends, brothers/sisters, boyfriends/girlfriends, teachers, school work, coaches, trainers, tutors and other appointments. If this sounds familiar, without a way to deal with these stressors, life can feel pretty difficult.

Most of us are also over-stimulated. For the most part, we are able to do so much more in a much shorter amount of time. We have Palm Pilots, iPods, PSPs, IMing, BlackBerries, iTunes, cell phones, MySpace or Facebook. The Internet connects us to so many more people and so much more information. Everybody is multi-tasking. Come on, you have probably been that person who works on homework while IMing people, surfing the Internet, downloading music and maybe even texting or talking on your cell phone all at the same time. Even news or music videos images don't stay on the screen for more than 10 seconds. The bottom line is that teen life is faster today than ever before. Many teens come into my office saying that they think they have ADD because they sit down in class and they just can't concentrate. Their mind just keeps moving and they have no idea what the teacher is talking about. The same thing happens to a helicopter when it's powered down after landing -- the engine is off but the blades just keep spinning and spinning.

You need stress-relief tools to help chill you out and bring you back to the present. Below are some techniques that will help you relax and refocus.

- <u>3x3x3 Breathing</u>
  Sit up straight and fill your lungs up with air with a three second inhale through your nose. Imagine that you are taking in pure, clean, cleansing air. It should be such a big breath that it makes your chest stick out. Hold it for three seconds. While you are doing this, imagine that all of what is stressing you out, hurting you or making you angry is accumulating as smoke in your lungs. Now blow it out through your mouth for three seconds. Get it out of your body and off of you. Do this two more times in a

row. This will take the edge off of anything that you are dealing with.

- Focus on Black

    Place the palms of your hands over your eyes. Do not push hard. Just hard enough to block out the light. Think only this to yourself: What does black look like? What does black smell like? What does black taste like? What does black sound like? What does black feel like? Incorporate every sense and just keep doing it over and over. You will block out the world, your thoughts and give yourself a few minutes of peace.

- Kneeling by a Stream

    Do some 3x3x3 breathing to relax yourself. Close your eyes and imagine that you are kneeling next you the most beautiful stream of water you have ever seen (real or imagined). Incorporate the senses. What does is look, smell, taste, feel, sound, like? Next, imagine that as you look at your feet you see leaves. Each leaf represents something that is stressing you out, hurting you or making you angry. Pick up a single leaf, imagine what it represents for you and then drop it into the moving water. Watch it spin, twirl, and get carried completely out of sight by the water. Then pick up another leaf, think to yourself what it represents and drop it in, watching it disappear. Do this until you feel you've gotten through the things bothering you.

- <u>Tense and Release</u>

  Start with tensing you toes as hard as you can for 5 seconds, then let go. Don't slowly let go, quickly let it go. Next, move up to your calves. Tense them for 5 seconds as hard as you can and quickly let it go. Do this with every single muscle group as you work your way up to your head. Don't forget your stomach, cheeks and forehead. This will help release your tension.

- <u>Hands on Shoulders</u>

  You know what your hands look like right? Have you ever have a killer neck massage where someone used their thumbs to massage the base of your neck and you got the tingles up your neck and back? When I get quickly stressed (like getting cut off by another car, or if somebody says or does something that angers me) I imagine my own hands coming up over my shoulders and my thumbs rubbing my neck. I feel an immediate small relief from it. If your younger brother or sisters start to bug you, someone cuts you off or if you just find yourself getting really angry really quickly, do this. You'll take the edge off and hopefully keep yourself in check.

- <u>Hitting Stuff</u>
  It is not good practice to get rid of tension by hitting things, or people for that matter. If it comes down to the point where you have to hit something because you are absolutely going to snap on someone, then hit your pillow or mattress. You probably have one, right? You've got to hit something that doesn't hurt property or others. If you grab your pillow, put it on your mattress and go to town on it, you shouldn't hurt yourself or

someone else. Again, this is NOT a good way to get rid of tension. The best thing you can do is talk about what is bothering you.

Feeling Even Better: Environmental Tools

GIVE OF YOURSELF

Everything that you do affects the people you are around and vice versa. It is like throwing a rock into a still pond. The ripples will eventually hit all sides of the pond. When I was feeling down, I would do nice things for people. This did a lot to pull me out of my tailspin. Instead of focusing on myself and my crappy situation, I began to focus on other people. I'd give a homeless guy $20, hold a door for someone, tell someone who looked like they were having a horrible day that I liked a piece of their clothing, let someone go in traffic.

Go figure, I started feeling better.

If you haven't figured this out already, life is about giving and making this world a better place, not about just taking what you can accumulate. Every time I've been selfish, my life has started going in the wrong direction. Every time I have given to others and worked to make this world a better place, amazing things have happened. I felt better, opportunities opened up. Life speaks to you if you pay attention. After being selfish and "a taker" and then seeing how I felt when I was the opposite, I realized that life was trying to tell me, "Jerry, go out and make a difference you fool!"   The ancient theory of karma seriously exists in life. It's the Golden Rule. As I've said before, what you give, you get back – both with people and with school work. Small things, when done for others, equal a great payoff for you. That is all there is to it. If you haven't figured this one out, you will. No joke.

YOU ARE YOUR SURROUNDINGS
Everybody has heard that you're a product of your environment, right? It is true. Is your room messy and unorganized right now? Is your car nasty? I

realized when I was depressed that I had crap everywhere and it was pulling me down. I started cleaning and organizing my place. I cleaned my car. I started feeling more together. It was also a more productive work environment. I've realized that if I'm feeling down and walk into a clean and organized room or car, I'm going to feel better. Conversely, if I walk into a dirty room when I'm feeling good, it is going to pull me down. Try it for yourself.

DRESS TO IMPRESS

When I was feeling depressed, I was looking for anything to help make me feel better. I tried dressing better. I started putting a little more effort into my appearance and I started feeling better. Dress up. Sometimes you can feel better when you are look good on the outside, too. Hook it up!

GET OUT AND ABOUT

I believe that humans are social animals by nature. We need to be around others, even if we don't know them. Just getting out and about makes you feel better. When I was depressed, I would get in my car and take off. Or I would crutch around outside. It was the closest thing I could do to going for a walk.

Just going to a park and being around people I didn't know elevated my mood. Seriously, get out of the house. The worst thing that you can do if you are not feeling good (or want to feel better) is stay inside alone.

AND EVEN BETTER YET: SOCIAL TOOLS

SAVE THE DRAMA

Seriously, how much drama is there in high school? Plenty! Do you ever wonder why? I was thinking about it and one factor is that no one really knows who they are, where they're going or what they'll become. This creates a state of insecurity, anxiety and drama. Even bigger, though, is that this is the first time that most people are having serious friendships and relationships with boyfriends or girlfriends.

With all the good stuff comes the flip-side of that – the negativity. This is the first time that many young adults deal with the fights, break-ups, hook-ups, cheating or betrayals. The first time you go through anything it is difficult. You might not remember this, but the first time you learned to swim, you were probably dropped into the pool with floaties on your arms and had a thought, "I'm going to drown in this pool!" But now you can swim. It's the same thing. That is partly why the OMG kids are running around going, "Oh my God, Oh my God, Oh my God!" This is not the first time that you are going to go through situations like this. As they happen more often, it gets easier and you will know more of what to expect. I swear.

THE REVOLVING DOOR OF FRIENDS

Friends come and friends go. That is just how it is. For most of you, the majority of people that you are friends with right now are not your friends from middle school, and your friends from middle school were probably not your friends from elementary school.

What's a friend? Someone with whom you see eye-to-eye and have a lot in common. As you continue to change, mature, and piece together who you are going to be in your future, so will your friends. Typically, you all don't end up in the exact same place. You don't see eye-to-eye as much anymore. That's O.K. I freaked out the first few times that I felt myself growing away from my friends. I was thinking about losing my friendships and it made me nervous and anxious. I over-thought situations and I lost sleep. But finally I figured out what was happening and made peace with it.

As you mature, you change and end up in different places. That's all there is to it. There are many other people that you will find with similar interests that will become better friends to you in the future. Don't sweat it.

Second, very few people find REAL friends as teenagers in high school. I define this as people that you love, that have your back at 4:00 in the morning, that treat you the same way you treat them. If you have that, you are stoked. Most teens don't though. Like we previously discussed, everybody is at a different stage of life.

High school is a time when most people are very self-absorbed and that is a tough way to have a two-way relationship where you find someone who puts your needs as close to the same level as you do their own. Girls gossip and guys bag on each other. This is why you usually have better and closer friends in college and the real world. Not only is everyone more mature, but they also begin to care more about others. By that time, many have figured out at that point how important it is to not just have friends and put maintenance into relationships, but also that what you give, you get back.

For the most part, I had lots of acquaintances that I called friends. You know, people to kick it with so that you are not alone, but not really your best friend either. If you are not digging your friends right now, don't worry, better relationships are coming.

YOU ARE WHO YOU HANG WITH

People - as we all know - make a lot of assumptions and pre-judge. Because of this, you will be considered "just like" the people you kick it with even if you are not. It just isn't like this in high school, but in college and the real world, too. Who are you currently hanging out with? Do they have your back and help to propel your life in the direction you are supposed to be going? Actions speak louder then words. Love and friendships are both BEHAVIORS. Many people in life will do something that hurts or offends you and say they're sorry, that they really care about you and will change, but keep doing the same thing over and over again.

Think about the relationships you are in right now with regards to the walk, not the talk. Are you getting what you need? Or are you just getting lip service? I have found that it is vital to surround yourself with positive, upbeat people who are genuine and who have your back. They will both support you and be a straight-shooter for you when you need it in life. This is what has helped me to become successful in life. Think of it as a sled-dog race. Are you going to select dogs that look good or that you'd want to like you? Or are you going to get the fastest ones around that will make you and your sled haul ass? As always, you are the one behind the wheel. Who do you want riding shotgun?

CAN THE JEALOUSY

Have you seen what is on T.V. today? Aside from its entertainment value, what can you take from the majority of shows? The messages that come from the majority of them are that you have to be good-looking, skinny, tan, have a six-pack, have a sweet house by the beach, be on T.V., have tons of cash, a really hot boyfriend/girlfriend, the latest Fendi bag, or a black Escalade with chrome 22"s and the in-dash DVD player to be someone worthy of status, love, attention and support?

What a crock.

Don't fall foolishly to the media machine that tells you what is hot right now and will make you popular. It's simply showing you fool's gold. You can sacrifice your whole life trying to accumulate all this stuff and still never be happy. It's YOUR life. Figure out for yourself what life is really all about. Be an independent thinker and make your own decisions. If you don't want your parents telling you how to live your life, then why would you let the media?

You stand to lose so much if you merely judge someone else by their exterior. Everybody has a soul. Your soul is who you are and your body is just your vehicle to get around life in. If you judge someone based on their race, ethnicity, color, religion, weight or height, then you don't see them, just their exterior.

Get to know the driver of the car, don't just judge someone by the car they drive. You could be missing out on one of the best friends of your life. Someone who would have your back at 4:00 in the morning when you need their support. Someone who you might have a ton in common with.

There is a huge difference between what you NEED and what you WANT. What you need is basic things like shelter, food, water, maybe some affection. That is all we really need and many teens out there aren't even getting that. If you are currently getting what you need in life to survive, try to find a way to be O.K. with that. Once you do, anything on top of that will seem like icing on the cake. If you can't reset your frame of reference, nothing will ever be enough and you will keep feeding that bottomless pit where no matter what you acquire, you still won't feel satisfied.

Jealousy is all-or-nothing. What I mean can be summed up in one question: Would you give up your parents, your brothers or sisters, your car, your dog, your aunt and uncles, your cousins, your grandparents, your house and your friends for all of anyone else's? Of course not. No matter how bad you have it, you still wouldn't trade it, right?

So what's up with picking out pieces? See, when you look at others and think "I want a car like that, I want legs like that, I want a girl like that, I want a house like that, I want a body like that, and I want a bag like that," you are looking for pieces, not a whole experience.

It's kind of like if you were driving down the freeway in your car and you see a brand new red Ferrari pull up next to you and thought you yourself "That is a sweet hood. I want a hood like that!" Then you go to a chop shop and put a red Ferrari hood on the front of your car. What do you think that would look like? It is the exact same thing when you are looking at pieces of what others have. You need to stop this thinking. It is all-or-nothing. If you chose all (rather than none), then make it that way.

A great quote that I really enjoy for this topic is, "You make a LIVING by what you GET, but you make a LIFE by what you GIVE AND LEAVE BEHIND." Go make a LIFE for yourself.

THINK ABOUT IT: COGNITIVE TOOLS

IT'S IN YOUR INTERPRETATION

If there is one way to trip yourself out, it is by overanalyzing what is going on in your head. Depression, stress and anxiety all begin with your interpretation of an event. If you think that you will be annoyed in a particular situation, then you'll be annoyed. If you think that a situation will be stressful or anxiety-provoking, then it will. If you think that you can't do something, then you won't.

When I was doing an internship working with schizophrenic patients in college, there was a patient in the program that had a perfectly working foot but was obsessed with the fact that it didn't or wouldn't work. Over time, her foot started to slightly curl up and become somewhat deformed. After awhile, she couldn't use her foot normally. Your body listens to your mind. It was crazy for me to see how powerful the mind is over the body.

One of the more common things I see in my practice is people thinking negatively about things. What you have to realize is that your interpretation of an event (how you see it) result in your thoughts about it. Your thoughts about it result in your feelings about it and your feelings about it result in how you react and respond. Whenever you are not in a good place, you will be able to link that negative feeling to something you are thinking. The only time you will feel something before you think it is if someone punches you or something else physical.

Consider some of the thoughts I hear teens say a lot:
"I suck."
"I can't take being around that person."
"This is going to be so gay."
"I must have done something wrong for someone to treat me like that."

Many teens that I have treated have a tendency to catastrophize. They think of the worst-case scenario of the situation they're struggling with. How do you know that is what the situation will be like? What if it doesn't turn out that way? Look at all the energy you've wasted and the stress you've caused.

There's a saying, "Cross that bridge when you come to it." Think about the worst of that situation ONLY if it actually happens. The negative thoughts have to stop. How does thinking like that help your situation at all? It doesn't. It only makes it worse. Whenever you catch yourself thinking like that, yell at yourself, "Stop!" Even if it is after the fact. Replace that thought with its exact opposite. If you catch yourself thinking, "I can't," stop and replace that thought with, "I can."

Your thoughts set the stage a lot of the time for what is going to happen and how you are going to respond in the future. The more optimistic you can be, the more you are hooking yourself up big picture.

In addition, if you are bumming out right now (or in the future), you have to remind yourself that this is TEMPORARY. When I was in difficult situations, sometimes it felt like life was always going to be that way. It is so not. Probably 99% of the negative situations you deal with will not be that way forever. It is important to remind yourself of this. It is a temporary situation.

Do You Have Control?

Another common issue I see in my practice is people trying to control things that they do not have control over. The same way that you are the driver of your car in life, everyone else around you is the driver of theirs. If you haven't figured this out yet, all you have control over in life is your actions and reactions to situations. Everything else is out of your control. The past is out of your control. Stay focused on the here and now. You can't control a brother, sister, boyfriend, girlfriend, neighbor or parent. Trying to control something that you don't have control over is like trying to put a square peg in round hole. The more you try, the more frustrated you are going to become.

Many people are resentful at parents or friends for not giving them enough of what they're looking for (love, attention, and validation). You need to make peace with this by realizing that what you are waiting around for and what you are angry about probably isn't going to change. What you are seeking probably doesn't exist in that person. Once you can accept this, it is easier to move on.

You can't control people and getting people to change is really hard. If the situation isn't going to change, then it has to be your action and reaction to things that change. You shouldn't be too bothered that a family member embarrasses you or that your friend always gossips. If you've seen it twice, logic says that it is going to happen again. Accept that this is the way that they are and that more than likely they will do what bothers you many times again in the future. You should anticipate and expect it when you are with them, and find a way to be O.K. with it. Otherwise you are just freaking out.

Life to me is like a huge river. We're all in it, getting carried downstream. We can swim to different places, but nevertheless, we're getting carried downstream and we can't do anything about it but to accept that this is how it is and make the best of it. Think to yourself, "Do I have control over this situation or not?" If you do, you have something to work with. If you don't, you have to give it away and make peace with it.

Here is a great tool that helped me "unplug" from trying to control things: We have already established that most things in life we don't have control over and that everyone is the driver of their own car, right? So imagine that you are driving down the freeway and around you are your family members, friends, boyfriend/girlfriend driving their own cars. If you try to control a brother, sister, friend, boyfriend/ girlfriend that would be like pulling up to that person, unbuckling your seatbelt, hanging out the window and trying to jump through the window into their car so that you can grab their steering wheel and control their car.

First of all, there is no way you'd jump out of your car at 70 miles per hour. Secondly, no one else would want you jumping into their lap in their own car. They'd be like, "What the hell are you doing here? Get out!" Your only other alternative is to hit the gas and pull ahead, hit the breaks and drop back, roll up the windows, turn up the music or do something that is in your control that will make it easier on you. I know it is tough when you see someone (especially someone that you care about) in trouble and want to help, but you need to understand what you can and cannot control.

EMBRACE LIFE'S DIFFICULTIES

Look, life can be difficult. Guess what? There are always going to be difficult times as long as you are alive. But that's no reason to feel depressed. Accepting this fact has definitely helped me out in my life. Think about it: you are born alone and you die alone. In your lifetime, the people you love and care about are going to get diseases and die. You rent this life, you don't own it. The landlord can come at anytime and evict you when ever he or she feels like it. Yeah, that is kind of negative but if you accept that this is how it is, it helps you in a number of ways.

First, if you accept that this is how some of life is, it makes it easier to deal with the hard stuff when it comes. You know how the flu shot has a little of the flu in it, but it helps our bodies defend against it? If you accept this fact of life, you won't be caught off guard when it happens. You'll never be that person who stands around and says, "I never thought this would or could happen to me!" It always can and if you are prepared, you can get through it.

Second, it makes you, "Carpe Diem!" (Seize the Day). When you realize that you have a limited amount of time here, it should make you want to squeeze the most out of life everyday and live every day as if it were your last because it just could be.

Life is a lot of peaks and valleys. It just isn't you that has felt like they're riding a roller coaster. We all are. You have ups and downs no matter who you are. It will always be this way. Whenever I am not in a valley, I am very appreciative of it particularly because I know that there are going to be many more difficult or challenging times in my future. If you are up on a peak or even if you are just not in a valley, be appreciative of how good you have it at that time.

I believe to some extent that life is cyclical, which means that you have an almost equal amount of easy and challenging days. Think about it like this: If you are someone who has had to deal with a lot of crap in life, then you've gotten a lot of your tough days out of the way.

Avoid the Pity Party

One thing that I was definitely guilty of back when I was depressed (and something that everybody does) was feeling sorry for myself and my situation. After some time, I realized that all I really was doing was wasting time and energy by feeling sorry for myself. It was doing nothing to help get me out of the situation.

Everybody has pity parties for themselves. Please realize that this does nothing to help get you out of your current situation, and in fact, it stresses your relationships with others. Have you ever been around a "Debbie Downer" before? It could be a friend, family, really anyone. You ask them how it's going and they reply with, "Oh my God," and then proceed to drop a 200-pound boulder into your arms by telling you about how horrible everything is. This in turn stresses you out because when you are around them, everything seems to be negative. Who wants to hear that all the time? This is how you affect the people around you when you are in this mode of self-pity.

Feeling sorry for yourself when things go wrong in your life is just like getting a flat tire on the freeway and pulling over and crying about it for a few days or weeks when you have a cell phone, AAA card, a jack and a spare tire—the tools you need—so that you can use to get your tire changed immediately and merge back onto the freeway of life. Life doesn't stop for your pity party. It's important to keep perspective and tackle your challenges instead of crying about them.

To avoid the pity party, I have learned to put my life into perspective. Putting situations into perspective is absolutely necessary in life. There is a lot of heaviness in our world today, such as the poverty and disease in Africa, the wars, battles and conflicts throughout the world that kill thousands and displace hundreds of thousands of families. What you have to realize is that at any given time in your life, there are millions of people your age across the world that would trade you in a heartbeat for what you've got on the worst day of your life. When they find out that you have shelter or that you get to go to school, or that you have not just food but a refrigerator, or that you have running water or even that you don't have to dig a hole in the ground to go to the bathroom, they'd say, "Oh, me! Pick me! I want that person's life! Please!" Like we talked about earlier, there is a huge difference between what you need and what you want. There are so many out there who struggle every day to get just what they NEED to survive. Keep it all in perspective.

LOOK FOR THE POSITIVE

No matter what you are doing in life, you are either helping or hurting yourself. When I was depressed, I found myself focusing on everything that sucked. This is a lot like the pity party described above. I really believe that we have two different sets of goggles that we can wear in life. We have positive and negative. The people who wear negative goggles only see all of the negative things in life. We have already discussed that life is tough and that there are a lot of negative things in life. Why would you want to see it all and focus on it? Those people who wear the positive goggles typically see the good and positive in life. One perspective is good for you, the other pulls you down.

One thing that I challenge you to do is to try to find the positive in every negative situation. From every negative situation in life, I believe that you can pull at least one positive out of it to make your life easier and yourself feel better. It will make you more resilient as time goes on. Think about it: What is the one positive that you can find? Hold on to that and always look for it.

PARENT YOURSELF

Part of being an adult is learning to emotionally nurture yourself. If you are fully dependent on others (siblings, friends, significant others, parents) then you'll always be let down. You'll be let down because of the simple fact that no one is in your head with you, so no one knows exactly what you want, when you want it or how you want it. Only YOU know what you want and you are the only one who can give it to yourself.

Has someone ever done or said something to you and you react in a really immature way? Of course.

We all do that at times. Because the first five years of our life are so important and defining of who we become, I believe that we all carry little kids inside of us. I do, your parents do, your teachers and grandparents do. Whenever that kid in us doesn't get enough love, attention or support, he or she will reach up and shake the bottom part of our steering wheel and we'll sit there in our own world wondering, "Why is my car going all over the road right now?"

You are old enough that you should be able to deal with the majority of things that happen in your life. Whenever you feel really anxious, depressed or stressed, it is not you the young adult but the kid in you who feels scared, inadequate, insecure, hurt or angry. No matter how good or how bad you've had it as a kid or as a teenager, you'll always have a part of you who needs his or her mommy and daddy. Even when they're gone, you'll still have a need to have their support, love and attention. You need to learn to parent yourself. Here's how:

You have a kid in you about two feet tall. If you imagine yourself as a young child, you have an idea of what his or her hair is like, what outfit they're wearing, and what shoes they sport. What you are imagining right now is the kid inside of you who desperately needs your mature love and support. Take all of your negative emotions and imagine placing them onto this little kid. Now you have a child looking at you who is scared, angry, anxious and depressed. If this were your son and daughter, how would you pick them up and hug them to make them feel better? Imagine doing this. Imagine what their hair smells like, what their squishy skin feels like, what their cheek feels like against your cheek. Now what would you tell your child if they felt that way? Maybe it is something like "It's O.K. I'm here for you. Don't worry. I'm here for you and I love you and everything is going to be okay." If you do this, you will notice that you begin to feel better. You are learning to love and support yourself.

So many things are going to occur in life that are out of our control and will knock you off balance. The quicker that you can get back into balance, the better you'll feel and the more effective you'll be in life, both for yourself and for those around you. There is a saying that if you can't take care of yourself, you can't take care of anything (or anyone) else in your life. This begins with making yourself a priority and emotionally nurturing yourself. This totally helped me out when I was depressed and continues to help me when I get into difficult situations.

FORGIVE YOURSELF FOR YOUR MISTAKES

You've got a lot of pressure on you. With all the difficult things in this world, the last thing anyone needs is to kick their own butt and make their life more difficult. This does absolutely nothing positive. There were times when I screwed up and got all over myself about it, but it did nothing to help me and it didn't change the likelihood that I wouldn't do it again. It just brought me down further. There will be plenty of negative things to deal with in life, you don't need and deserve any more. I see so many teens that are so hard on themselves that they put themselves in situations where they become more anxious, more depressed and their self-esteem plummets. Mistakes and screw-ups are actually really good for you in life and a very important part of growing into an adult. Think about it, we all learn so much more from our mistakes in life than from our successes. Mistakes are really opportunities for growth and maturity.

When I was a teenager, I thought I knew all about life. I made a lot of mistakes and when I got to college, I realized I still didn't know that much. Now I'm in the real world and I still don't feel as though I've arrived. I don't think you ever really do.

And face it: You'll never stop making mistakes. When you screw up, ask yourself if you intentionally tried to do it. Did you wake up that morning and say to yourself, "I'm going to go screw myself over today?" Of course not. Then forgive yourself for your screw-up! Forgive yourself and learn from your mistakes or you'll make them again and many will be worse the next time. Pay attention to what life is trying to tell you. Learn, change, mature and move on.

DON'T GIVE UP

You have to be a fighter in life. The situations that come at you are simply hurdles that you have to rise above. Just like my lackluster SAT scores, there are hurdles big and small that we have to overcome in order to find success and happiness. I see so many young adults who come in to my office deflated, helpless, and who have given up. If some guy in a van pulled up to you while you were walking down the street and tried to grab you and throw you in the back, what would you do? You'd fight, right? What if the same guy tried to do the same thing every day between when you left the house and when you came back from school? Would you ever just give in and let him grab you and toss you in the back? Never. The situations that happen in life are not much different. Do not give up. You have to be a fighter in life to not only survive but to be successful.

How Emotions and Expression Work

Part of being an adult is learning to understand how emotions work and how to appropriately communicate. All emotions come from hurt and pain. If I had a pot of boiling hot potatoes and I took some tongs and tossed one into your lap, what would you do? Would you let it sit there? No! You'd toss it off, stand up, maybe throw it back at me, right? You'd protect yourself from the physical pain. Well, the same things happen with emotional hot potatoes. Friends, family, boyfriends/girlfriends and coaches are throwing hot potatoes into your lap and many of you just hold them. They don't lose their heat and they continue to burn you until you get them off of you. The way you get them off of you is by expressing yourself.

One way that you can express yourself and get things off of you is by talking about it. Talk about it with friends, family, parents or a therapist. Anyone. Just make sure that you don't dump too much on the same person or you'll stress your relationship with that individual.

Crying about it is the second way to express yourself. Allowing yourself to breakdown is actually one of the most effective and healthiest ways to express emotion and relieve issues. Guys, real men DO cry. It is just taking care of your business that's all. If you are one of those people who don't cry much, whenever you do, think of all the other things that are bothering you that you could cry about and get them out through the opening, as well.

The third way to express yourself is by writing about it. Get out a lined piece of paper and write about everything that you are thinking and feeling. It might be one page, it might be 20 pages. Like I said before, when you are done, shred it and get rid of it. You don't need to review it or have others read it. I also see many teens that write song lyrics, write poetry, draw or sculpt. All of these will help you to express your emotions and make you feel better.

Here's the thing, if you don't express your hurt it turns to anger. Think about anytime you've been angry. I guarantee that you were hurt first every single time. Anger stems from unexpressed hurt. People who have "anger management problems" like that guy that emotionally or physically bullies people at school or that girl who constantly gossips, they are all people who are not big intimidating people. They are actually small, hurt people who feel an inch tall.

If you don't express your anger, you get depressed. The anger in you will begin to build and make you feel worse about yourself. Repressing your feelings can result in psychosomatic problems. These are physical ailments with no medical explanation for them. Examples of these include: headaches, backaches, neck aches, stomach aches, diarrhea, and general body pain.

On top of that, if you keep stuffing your emotions, there is little room for the small things in life with parents, friends, siblings, boyfriends and girlfriends. Something small happens and you snap and explode. The people around you look at you like you are a totally out-of-control freak and you feel like it, too. This will contribute to depression. The more this goes on, the more you can develop anxiety.

What is anxiety really? It's the fear of future hurt or pain. That's it. There are so many people paralyzed by anxiety in their lives. The more you run away from or avoid what you are afraid of, the worse the fear perceptually becomes. The only way to get over it is to place yourself in the situation that you are scared of until your brain recalibrates itself and you realize that you were freaking out for nothing.

You already have what it takes to deal with the situation and be successful in life. The problem is that we're trained to listen to our brain. It is a survival mechanism. If you get burned by the stove, when you are around it the next time, your brain tells you stay away from that stove. It is trying to keep you from harm. If you have anxiety, this is the hardest part -- not listening to your brain, the feelings that go with it and pushing through what you are afraid of so that your brain can recalibrate itself and you can feel O.K. again.

When expressing your hurt, anger and anxiety, it is important to use "I feel" statements. When you talk about how you feel rather than lashing out at someone, not only are you acting like an adult, but you are also facilitating an actual adult conversation. If you just lash out at someone, their first response is going to be to shut down and defend themselves. They're not going to hear what you are saying and they will become defensive. I'm sure you've had plenty of conversations like this. They go absolutely nowhere and everybody is more upset at the end of it than at the beginning. Since everything comes from hurt, then you need to express what has hurt you. Here's an example: "It really hurt me that you treated me like that because I wouldn't treat you that way."

It is also important that the other person feels understood and heard. This can be accomplished by simply taking their perspective. "If I were in your shoes, I would feel upset, angry and belittled and I'm sorry I made you feel that way." It is hard for people to continue punishing or guilt tripping you if they know that you get it.

It is that easy.

OLE YELLER

Sometimes you are trying to express yourself to a "yeller." You know, those people start screaming the minute they get upset. It gets you even more charged up and before you know it, you are both screaming at each other. Understand that, though pretty ineffective, their yelling is an attempt to communicate. If you drop your voice much lower (like to the point of a whisper) and keep talking on that level with them even though they're still yelling, they will gradually lower their voices. This happens for two reasons: Your voice is calming them down and they're also legitimately trying to communicate. To continue, they have to lower their voices to somewhere near your level. Whether it's with your siblings, parents or friends, lower your emotion level and your voice. Make the conversation and everybody else in the environment less stressed and anxious. So much more information can be exchanged when people are acting rational and mature.

EXPRESS YOURSELF

Expressing yourself and being vulnerable with friends and family members can be intimidating for you as well as for the people you are expressing yourself to. Many are taught that expressing yourself honestly can be mean or critical and shouldn't be done because it might be hard to take and hurt somebody's feelings. That's simply not true. Expressing yourself is healthy and mature as long as you are doing it in an appropriate way. It's not just what you say but how you say it.

The "sandwich technique" of expressing yourself will make these conversations easier for everyone involved. Here's how it works: The two pieces of bread are positives and the "meat" in the middle is the hard issue you need to express. An example of this would be "Dad, I want you to know that I love you and care about you (top piece of bread), but when you tease me in front of Jenny it really hurts and embarrasses me (the meat). Please do not do it anymore. I'm only telling you this because I care about you and want to continue to have a good relationship with you (the bottom piece of bread)." It's easy to deliver and easy to receive.

Expressing yourself is obviously extremely important. Don't worry about how the people who hurt you react to it. You are doing this to get the "hot potato" off of you. Who cares where it goes? If you tell the person who hurt you that they hurt you, you will feel better. Even if they say "I don't care if I hurt you, I'm not wrong," you'll still feel better because you are not holding their hot potato for them anymore.

Do not stuff your issues. They will pull you down in other ways other than being depressed, anxious, and hot-tempered. People who "stuff" also get psychosomatic problems. Don't do this to yourself. Realize that expressing yourself helps with communication and helps another individual understand where you stand and what you are about. This will help you to have a better relationship with anyone. Act like an adult, express yourself and move on. I wish I had known how important and valuable this was earlier in my life.

GETTING ALONG WITH THE PARENTALS

Look, living with your parents is sometimes really difficult. If you are not happy with something, express yourself. If they still continue to do what bothers you, you really need to learn to accommodate yourself to their situation. I see so many young adults in my practice that keep fighting their parents, which only makes life much worse for them. I always say, "Don't bite the hand that feeds you, give it a massage instead."

Learn how to play the game. If you dig in on your parents, they are only going to dig in on you. Adapt to their situation. What they want from you is not going to change and you should try to accommodate them. This is a survival mechanism and it is only temporary. Your whole life will not be this way but it definitely will be better for you while you are in this situation. Accommodation and adaptation have been part of survival forever. Could you imagine if a chameleon turned neon red while sitting on a green bush when its predators were close instead of blending into its environment? Go with the flow. Remember: you are the one that wins, not them.

NOW TAKE ACTION!

So, we've talked about a lot of stuff. Unfortunately, there is no one person, pill, drink or even tool that will just make life 100% awesome when you are bumming out. My promise to you is that if you utilize many of the tools discussed in this book, you'll feel at least a little better regardless of whether your situation changes or not.

As you start your journey, try to remember the following:

SMALL THINGS MAKE A BIG DIFFERENCE

If you are ready to turn over a new leaf and want some help, all you need to do is change things up and rearrange your life. Because of conditioning, your habits, routines and the environment of your room pull you back to who you used to be rather than who you want to become. Rearrange the furniture in your room, paint, put up new posters.

Get a new haircut or change your style of clothing. Do what you can to bring the "new you" to the table. Think of whom you see yourself being in the future and start to step in to those shoes right now. How do you want the world to view you? When people hear your first and last name, what do you want them to think about? Spend some time really thinking about this.

EXPECT SETBACKS

Habits are really hard to break. You can really get fired up about doing things differently only to find it is one step forward and two steps back at first. This is not because you are a failure or because you suck. It's simply a habit that you have and habits are hard (but very possible) to break. If you don't get down on yourself when you take a step backwards, then you'll begin to take two or three steps forward with only one step back. The biggest thing is not to get down on yourself when you are trying to change things up even if you have a few setbacks, especially in the beginning.

Momentum Will Get You Somewhere

There is negative and positive momentum in life. Life is never static. You never stay in one place. You are either hooking yourself up and spiraling upwards, or you are making your life more difficult and doing the downward spiral that we are all so accustomed to. If you begin to be positive during negative situations, control what you can and let go what you cannot, learn to accept, love and support yourself and the kid in you, organize your life, get daily exercise, communicate and express emotions, give to and focus on others, eat well, get outside and get sun, sleep well, hold yourself with good posture, smile, surround yourself with good people who are going places and have your back, stop comparing yourself to others, accept that life is difficult, stop feeling sorry for yourself, and forgive yourself for your mistakes then you will be fine in life and any situation you deal with will not be as bad. This is my promise to you.

If I can "make it" with what I have started with, then there is no reason you can't. This is YOUR LIFE and it is YOUR show. You are the one in control. I wish you all the best on your journey and know that no matter what has happened or where you currently are in your life right now, that you deserve the best YOU can give yourself. Squeeze the nectar from life! Don't let your sweet ride rust in the driveway. Wash it, wax it, get the oil changed, fill it with gas, get in, roll down the windows, crank the music, grab the steering wheel and punch the frickin' gas! Be responsible and enjoy what you can in your life for as long as it lasts.

Life is too short for anything else.